W9-BLC-819

YOU KNOW YOUR CHILD IS GIFTED WHEN...

A BEGINNER'S GUIDE TO LIFE ON THE BRIGHT SIDE

Judy Galbraith, M.A.

Illustrated by Ken Vinton, M.A.
Edited by Pamela Espeland

free spirit
PUBLISHING®
Works
for kids®

Text copyright © 2000 by Judy Galbraith
Illustrations copyright © 2000 by Ken Vinton

Library of Congress Cataloging-in-Publication Data

Galbraith, Judy.
        You know your child is gifted when . . . a beginner's guide to life on the bright
    side / Judy Galbraith ; illustrated by Ken Vinton ; edited by Pamela Espeland.
            p.   cm.
    Includes bibliographical references and index.
    ISBN 1-57542-076-7 (pbk.)
        1. Gifted children. 2. Gifted children—Education. 3. Child rearing. I. Espeland,
    Pamela. II. Title.
    HQ773.5 .G37 2000
    649'.155—dc21   00-037168

Cover and interior design by Percolator
Index prepared by Randl Ockey

10 9 8 7 6 5 4 3 2
Printed in Canada

Free Spirit Publishing Inc.
217 Fifth Avenue North, Suite 200
Minneapolis, MN 55401-1299
(612) 338-2068
help4kids@freespirit.com
www.freespirit.com

ACKNOWLEDGMENTS

Special thanks to Betty Johnson, a parent, grandparent, and long-time educator and advocate for gifted children, who read this book in its early stages and offered thoughtful and helpful comments.

I'm grateful to the parents who shared stories about their gifted children and gave me permission to print them here. Although I wasn't able to use every story, I read and appreciated them all. My thanks go out to Tonya Andersen, Hilary Cohen, Lee and Dana Dugatkin, Kathy A. Eads, Pamela Espeland, Karla Evans, Christine Fessler, Nancy Golon, Leese Johnson, Kiesa Kay, Carolyn Kottmeyer, Joni Lawver, Wendy Lestina, Kiki Mercer, Lisa Rivero, Mike Robinson, Teresa M. Schultz-Jones, Michelle Smith, Elizabeth Verdick, Erin Vienneau, Meredith Warshaw, Gayle Wiens, and Kathy Zappa.

CONTENTS

INTRODUCTION

John was driving to the store with his son, Lars.

"Dad," Lars asked, "if there's no air in space, how does the sun burn?"

"You don't need oxygen for a nuclear reaction," John responded.

"Oh, that's right," said Lars. "I forgot."

Lars was 4.

All kids say and do cute and wonderful things. All parents have stories they love to tell about their children—times when they were surprised, delighted, or left speechless. As a teacher, author, publisher, speaker, and workshop presenter, I've heard many tales of accomplishments, achievements, and amazing feats. But the ones about gifted kids stand out.

I've worked with, taught, and been an advocate for gifted children and teens for more than 20 years. During that time, I've talked with countless parents. One question I'm asked over and over again is, "I think my child is gifted, but how can I be sure?" In fact, if you think your child is gifted, you're probably right. You know your child better than anyone, and you're in the best position to judge your child's abilities and potential. In one study, a researcher found that parents were *better* at identifying giftedness than teachers.

Officially, and usually for purposes of deciding which kids will get into special school programs, "giftedness" is determined by screening and assessment. Most often, this involves tests, observations (by testers, teachers, and counselors), and reviewing the child's school performance. This book can't assess your child, but it can give you insights into what it means to be gifted, why it matters to know if your child is gifted, and what to do if he or she is gifted. You'll discover some of the most commonly accepted characteristics of giftedness, along with some of the good things (and not-so-good things) about each one. You'll uncover some myths, find answers to frequently asked questions, and benefit from the wisdom of experts—including parents like you.

Please keep five things in mind while you read:

1. It's very rare for one person to have *all* of the characteristics and traits of giftedness described here. Your child might exhibit several or a few.

2. When defining the characteristics, I alternate between "he" and "she." This reinforces the fact that these characteristics apply to girls and boys alike, and it makes for easier reading than "he or she."

3. Children used to start school at age 5, when they entered kindergarten. Today, many children are in day care as infants and toddlers, and in Head Start and preschool before kindergarten. Structured learning begins at an early age. Rather than use the words "day care or preschool or school," I've simplified to "school." And "teacher" means any kind of teacher—kindergarten, elementary, preschool, or day-care provider.

4. Some of the language used in this book may seem like academic jargon. I've tried to keep this to a minimum, but sometimes a particular word or phrase is the best, most accurate way to name or describe something. Also, it's important for you to know these words and phrases. Many day-care providers, teachers, and administrators use them. If you understand them, too, you'll be more prepared and confident as you meet with educators to talk about your child.

5. There's a reason why this book is called "a beginner's guide." It's not the last word on giftedness, and it doesn't cover everything there is to know about gifted children. (That would take a library of books!) When you want to find out more, please see the Resources on pages 109–115.

I hope you'll learn something new from reading this book. Chances are, it will confirm what you already know (or at least suspect): that you have a gifted child—with all the ups and downs, joys and challenges that brings. It's also my hope that this book will help you help your child. Of all the people in your child's life, now and in the years ahead, you're the one whose love, support, and understanding matter most. I wish you well.

Judy Galbraith

Judy Galbraith, M.A.

YOU KNOW YOUR CHILD IS GIFTED WHEN...

He knows everything there is to know
about giraffes...and chess, and Top 40 music,
and Humphrey Bogart movies.

ADVANCED INTELLECTUAL ABILITY

(REALLY, REALLY SMART)

This is the trait most people think of when they hear the word "gifted." A child with advanced intellectual ability may:

- seem just plain smart in a lot of areas, including some that might surprise you
- easily grasp new ideas and concepts
- understand ideas and concepts more deeply than other children his age
- come up with new ideas and concepts on his own, and apply them in creative and interesting ways
- easily memorize facts, lists, dates, and names
- have an excellent memory and never forget a thing ("But Mo-om, you promised!")
- learn new materials (and learn to use new things) more easily and quickly than other children his age
- really *love* to learn—which may or may not include loving school (more about that later)
- enjoy playing challenging games and making elaborate plans— the more complex, the better

- have friends who are older (because he needs someone to match wits and interests with)
- enjoy books, movies, games, and activities meant for older children or even adults
- know many things that other children his age seem totally unaware of

At the beginning of the first grade, Raoul drew a life-sized self-portrait and presented it to his teacher. She was puzzled, so he explained that it was a self-portrait "without his skin on." She said it looked messy, so he went back to his work table to simplify it. When he brought it to her again, he had color-coded the nervous, skeletal, and muscular systems in red, blue, and black.

GOOD THINGS: A smart child is a source of pride. Plus it's fun to have a brain and use it. Being able to learn, understand, and remember many things is a definite advantage. Intelligent children are good problem solvers, and they seek new challenges—which can lead to a more interesting life. And, though it sometimes seems that the only people we look up to are athletes and other celebrities, smart people are often accomplished, respected, and admired.

NOT-SO-GOOD THINGS: A brainy child might be easily bored, especially in school. Sometimes a child with a smart mind also has a smart mouth. He might act like a show-off and a know-it-all. He might have problems getting along with others who feel intimidated by his knowledge. He might be impatient with others who seem "slow" to him. Rapid learning can lead to inaccuracy and sloppiness when little hands can't keep up with speedy thoughts. Or a child might get impatient with one thing ("I already know that!") and want to move on, even if he's still working on an assignment, task, or project. Plus being really smart can complicate life with more choices, more interests, more possibilities—and more pressures.

ways to help Your BRainy child

1. Feed that hungry young mind. Make lots of books and magazines available. Take frequent trips to the library. Find family-friendly Web sites to surf together. Visit museums, go to concerts, go to movies, travel if you can. And talk, talk, talk.

2. Be a learner yourself. Show by example that learning is something people can and should do every day of their lives, not just when they're in school.

3. Keep track of your child's school performance and progress. Ask about his experiences and listen to his stories. You'll be able to tell if your child is happy in school or bored, busy learning or frustrated.

4. Stay in touch with your child's teacher. Attend parent-teacher conferences. (Ask if your child can come, too. Why not, if the conference is about him?) Do your part to build a courteous, respectful relationship. That way, if problems arise, it will be easier to work together to find solutions. *Tip:* Notice when the teacher is doing a good job. A thank-you note, friendly telephone call, or positive comment during a conference goes a long way.

5. Help your child learn and practice social skills. Encourage him to recognize and appreciate other people's talents. If his classmates and other kids his age don't share his interests and abilities, look for groups, organizations, and special classes where he can meet people who do.

MYTH: Being gifted guarantees straight A's in school.

FACT: Being smart (even really, really smart) doesn't always lead to high grades. Some highly gifted children don't do well in school at all. Then again, there are gifted kids who get A's but aren't learning anything because they already know all or most of what's being covered. So their grades don't show progress, just performance.

What does "gifted" mean?

It used to mean that the child tested in the top five percent of the population on general intelligence tests. Today we know that giftedness is more than an IQ score, so the definition is much broader.

Here's the latest federal definition—the one that reflects current knowledge and thinking:*

> "Children and youth with outstanding talent perform or show the potential for performing at remarkably high levels of accomplishment when compared with others of their age, experience, or environment.

> "These children or youth exhibit high performance capability in intellectual, creative, and/or artistic areas, possess an unusual leadership capacity, or excel in specific academic fields. They require services or activities not ordinarily provided by the schools.

> "Outstanding talents are present in children and youth from all cultural groups, across all economic strata, and in all areas of human endeavor."

---

* U.S. Department of Education, *National Excellence: A Case for Developing America's Talent*, Washington, DC: 1993.

You probably noticed that this definition doesn't use the word "gifted." Many organizations, schools, and individuals aren't comfortable with that word and avoid it whenever they can. They think it's elitist—that it defines a certain group as being better than everyone else. They worry that it's unfair to those who might not have outstanding talents or abilities. Some adults describe giftedness as a *disability* to avoid offending people who aren't gifted (or whose children aren't gifted).

On the other hand, many organizations, schools, and individuals do use the word "gifted." It's simple, straightforward, and clear. If the point is to support bright, talented kids—not hold them back—why not call them "gifted"? And also make it clear that being gifted is a good thing? It's hurtful when kids with remarkable abilities are made to feel ashamed or apologetic, as if they should hide their true selves in order to fit in.

"Arguments of elitism are foolish. This nation fosters a sense of elitism when it comes to sports or the entertainment industry. Certainly there needs to be no apology for those who wish to nurture the minds of the best young students." —JAMES BRAY

OTHER WORDS FOR "GIFTED"
(And Why They're Not as Good)

Gifted children are called many things. This can get confusing for parents (and even more confusing for kids). Some of these terms describe only part of what it means to be gifted, and others mean something different today than they used to. Here's a short list of words that are used instead of "gifted," with reasons why "gifted" is usually a better choice.

Genius: Once in wide use, now used only for the super-gifted—people like Einstein, Marie Curie, Stephen Hawking, and Marilyn vos Savant.

Talented: Refers to a particular strength or ability (for example, a talent in music, leadership, or math). Gifted kids usually have many talents, not just one.

Prodigy: Describes someone with an advanced skill that emerges at an early age (for example, a violin prodigy, math prodigy, tennis prodigy, or chess prodigy). Gifted kids often have many skills, and they might emerge early or later.

Precocious: Usually refers only to young gifted children.

Superior: A comparative term. Superior to what? To whom? A gifted child might be superior to most children his age in some ways (for example, verbal skills), but inferior in other ways (for example, motor skills). Plus this is a word that makes a lot of people uncomfortable.

High IQ: Another comparative term. Higher than what? Plus it's limiting. Giftedness is more than a number or a test score.

Rapid learner: This is just one characteristic of giftedness. It helps us understand giftedness, but it's not the whole story.

Exceptional: Once used to describe children who were "different" because they were smarter than average. Today it's also used to describe children with disabilities. Giftedness is not a disability.

Elite: This used to be a positive term, but not anymore.

Adapted from "Giftedness and the Gifted: What's It All About?" ERIC Clearinghouse on Handicapped and Gifted Children, Reston, VA; EC Digest #476, 1990.

Where does giftedness come from?

There will be days when you think to yourself, "What a terrific kid—and to think he's MY kid!" And days when you groan inwardly and think, "Is it MY fault that my child is such a pain in the behind?"

Giftedness is part *nature* (inherited from parents or grandparents) and part *nurture* (day-to-day interactions with people and things around us). You can't do anything about the nature part of your child's gifts, but you can affect the nurture.

Spend time together with your child learning, exploring, and playing. Keep lots of books and other reading materials around the house. (Isn't it great that public libraries are free?) Limit exposure to TV and computer games. Provide ample opportunities for enrichment—going deeper into subjects that interest your child, or working on higher-level skills. Make your child's environment a place where he learns and grows, blossoms and thrives in the care of loving, encouraging adults.

YOU KNOW YOUR CHILD IS GIFTED WHEN...

Your 5-year-old asks for an
unabridged dictionary for her birthday.

VERBAL PROFICIENCY

(WORDS, WORDS, WORDS)

This is one of the most obvious signs that a child is gifted. Suddenly she's speaking in complete sentences or using words you didn't know she knew. A verbally proficient child may:

- talk early (and never stop talking!)
- skip the period of grammatical errors ("I falled," "he gots") that most toddlers go through
- pronounce words correctly from the start
- quickly develop a large and advanced vocabulary
- use complex sentence structure (conjunctions like "however" and "although")
- make up elaborate stories
- easily memorize poems and stories
- enjoy reciting poems and rhymes
- prefer books with more words and fewer pictures
- catch you if you skip parts of books you're reading aloud to her
- teach herself to read by asking questions ("What's this letter?" "What's this word?"), watching TV, and/or hearing the same books read aloud several times

- read early and progress rapidly
- enjoy playing with words and inventing words
- easily and spontaneously describe new experiences
- give complex answers to questions (even simple questions)
- explain her ideas in complex and unusual ways
- have an early interest in printing letters, names, and words

Olivia was speaking in sentences at a year and a half. By age 2, when playing with children her age, she'd ask her parents, "Why don't they talk to me?" Her long, involved, made-up stories already included words like "difficult," "arrange," "ignoring," "disgusting," "appreciate," and "serious." Her friends didn't talk to her because they didn't yet have the words to converse at her level—a fact her parents found hard to explain.

GOOD THINGS: It's wonderful to have a child who can express herself clearly, colorfully, and eloquently. This is a child you can really talk to! Plus communication skills are important to success in school and in life.

NOT-SO-GOOD THINGS: A child with high verbal ability might have trouble making friends with children her age, simply because other kids don't understand what she's saying. This might be a child who learns early to manipulate other people with words, or who uses language to show her superior intelligence and ability. Plus what if she never shuts up?!?!?

ways to help your CHATTY child

1. Encourage your child's verbal gifts. Choose more challenging books to read aloud. If she's reading on her own, provide books, magazines, newspapers—whatever she wants (within appropriate limits). Make sure she has her own library card, and visit the library often.

2. Take this opportunity to build *your* vocabulary. Learn new words together.

3. Help your child find friends she can talk to. Look for classes, play groups, and hobby groups. Where to start? Ask your child's teacher or the school's gifted coordinator.

4. Teach your child how to be a good listener. Here are the basics: Look at the speaker. Sit up or stand up straight. Don't fidget or act bored. Show that you're paying attention. Nod and respond verbally ("Really?" "That's great!" "What happened next?" "Wow!").

5. Build some quiet time into your day. You and your child might sit side-by-side reading, coloring, thinking, or whatever—but no talking! If you have a gabby gifted child, you need this daily break.

During a trip to the bookstore with her parents, Jessie, 3½, pulled a "Bob Book" from the shelf and started reading it aloud. Her parents had no idea that she knew how to read.

Are gifted kids really that different?

Yes. They really are. They're often so much *more* of everything than other kids their age—more intense, curious, challenging, frustrating, sensitive, passionate. They *know* so much more. They *learn* so much faster. They *feel* so deeply.

Think about what it means to read at age 4, for example. Not only do you have a skill that most other kids your age don't have, but reading changes your life forever. You have access to information and ideas, stories and fictional characters. Your world broadens beyond your family, school, and community. You're exposed to the thoughts, feelings, and imaginations of adult writers from other times and places. As a result, your thinking skills race ahead of other children your age. Reading isn't just a skill, like tying your shoes. It's a profound awakening.

What does it mean to have an advanced vocabulary? You soon discover that you can't communicate with kids your age. And what if you're just plain smarter than most other kids you know—or more curious, energetic, focused, complex, and/or creative? Any and all of these qualities set you apart. You know it, and so do the people around you. You act differently. Others treat you differently. They expect more of you. Or they tease you for being different.

The sooner you accept and welcome the fact that your child isn't like other kids, the happier you'll both be. And the more you'll be able to help your child.

★ ★ ★

"Many parents and teachers would like the gifted child to be perfectly 'normal' in every way except the ability to perform academic tasks. Life would be so much easier that way. Over and over we see in media reports on gifted and highly gifted kids the assurance that (except for taking college courses in calculus while in the eighth grade) this child is just like everybody else. Even those who work in gifted education often spend a great deal of time and energy assuring people that gifted children are children first and gifted only secondarily, that they're 'just kids' who need a little extra challenge in school. This is simply not the case. Though they are clearly children, with children's needs for play, nurturing, structure and exploration, they have definite differences.... As the developmental trajectory diverges from the norm (very early in life) it takes on a unique shape that will remain unique." —STEPHANIE TOLAN

★ ★ ★

BRIGHT VS. GIFTED

The bright child...	The gifted child...
Knows the answers.	Asks the questions.
Is interested.	Is extremely curious.
Pays attention.	Gets involved physically and mentally.
Works hard.	Plays around, still gets good test scores.
Answers questions.	Questions the answers.
Enjoys same-age peers.	Prefers adults or older children.
Is good at memorizing.	Is good at guessing.
Learns easily.	Is bored. Already knew the answers.
Listens well.	Shows strong feelings and opinions.
Is self-satisfied.	Is highly critical of self (perfectionistic).

"The Gifted and Talented Child," written by Janice Szabos, Maryland Council for Gifted & Talented, Inc., PO Box 12221, Silver Spring, MD 20908. Reprinted by permission.

YOU KNOW YOUR CHILD IS GIFTED WHEN...

He has already asked "Why?" 100 times today...
and it's only 8:00 in the morning.

CURIOSITY

(ENDLESS QUESTIONS)

If a child is very smart, chances are he'll also be very curious. And if he has strong verbal skills, he'll use them to satisfy his curiosity. Gifted kids want to know something about everything (and everything about some things), and they're not shy about asking. Their insatiable curiosity can delight and frazzle their parents, teachers, and other adults. A curious child may:

- ask a lot of questions—one after another
- want to know about abstract ideas like love, relationships, feelings, justice, time, and space ("When is today really tomorrow or yesterday?")
- ask tough questions ("Why do people have to go hungry?" "Why are there wars?" "Why are some species endangered?")
- really listen and process the answers (which means you can't just toss something off without thinking about it, or you *will* be challenged)
- have a wide range of interests
- move quickly from one interest to another
- enjoy trying new things
- enjoy doing many things

24

When Matt was 7, his parents bought him a science encyclopedia. It was 700 pages long and written at a middle-school level. Matt insisted that the encyclopedia be his "bedtime story" until his father had read the whole thing from cover to cover.

GOOD THINGS: Curious kids are fun to be around. They keep you on your toes. They're eager to learn, and they'll ask almost anything—which is how learning happens.

"Satisfaction of one's curiosity is one of the greatest sources of happiness in life." —LINUS PAULING

NOT-SO-GOOD THINGS: These children can make you feel crazy with their never-ending whys, whens, what fors, what ifs, whos, and how comes. Some of their questions might seem embarrassing. And they can run you ragged as they veer wildly from one interest to another.

ways to help Your CURIOUS child

1. Create a home library of reference books—a dictionary, thesaurus, world almanac, book of world records, book of facts, book of quotations, and one-volume encyclopedia, for starters. Add reference books on topics that interest your child—stars, cars, dinosaurs, or whatever. If you have a home computer, get an encyclopedia on CD-ROM. If you have an Internet connection, explore online encyclopedias (like Britannica.com, Encyclopedia.com, and FunkandWagnalls.com).

2. When your child asks a question you can't answer, say so. (By admitting you don't know everything, you're setting a good example.) Then try to find the answer together—by going to the library, searching the Internet, making phone calls, and/or asking experts on the subject.

3. What if the question doesn't have an answer? You might say, "You know, that's a great question. A lot of people wonder about the same thing, and I'm not sure anyone has come up with an answer. What do *you* think the answer might be?" Then share your thoughts, too.

4. Learn to tell the difference between questions your child cares about and those he's asking for fun, out of boredom, or to drive you crazy. You might ask him, "Is this something you really need to know, or can it wait?"

5. Be curious yourself. Let your child know when you're learning something new, following an interest, or hunting down the answer to a question you've been wondering about.

How are gifted kids identified?

"Identification" is a word you may hear often, especially as your child moves through school. It describes the process used to select kids with ability or potential for gifted programs—when and where such programs are available (they aren't always). Identification is based on one or more of the following:

- group or individual intelligence tests (IQ tests)
- standard achievement tests
- creativity tests
- grades
- teacher observations
- parent recommendations

Note: It's always better and more accurate to combine several ways instead of using just one (for example, IQ tests alone). Also, the way children are identified for a particular gifted program should reflect the program's focus. For example, if a program is very academic, a creativity test isn't the best choice. If the program involves lots of hands-on creative or inventive activities, an IQ test might not find the right kids.

why these methods aRen't peRfect

IQ tests might fail to catch gifted kids who don't read well, whose life experiences have been different from many of the other children in their school, and/or who are having a bad day. Individual tests are more accurate than group tests, but they're also more costly and time-consuming, so they're not widely used. Also, different districts have different cutoff points for acceptance into gifted programs. For some, it's a 125 IQ; for others, it's a 145 IQ. Twenty points is a big gap.

IQ BREAKDOWN

Strictly FYI (For Your Information), here are some of the most commonly used IQ score categories. **Note:** There are several different versions of this breakdown, so don't assume this is the one your child's school will use.

IQ Score	Category
180+	Profoundly gifted (about 1 in 1,000,000)
160	Exceptionally gifted (about 1 in 100,000)
145	Highly gifted (about 1 in 1,000)
130	Gifted
115	Bright
100	Upper normal
85	Lower normal

Achievement tests measure what someone knows and can do, not what his potential might be. And they only test up to a certain "ceiling" or level. *Tip:* If you think your child is beyond other children his age, you might ask if he can be tested with kids a grade or two ahead.

Creativity tests are good at catching gifted children who might slip through the IQ test net. But they aren't used very often and might not be available at your child's school.

"Test scores should never 'define' a person, no matter what they may reveal about his or her intellectual or achievement potential. No single test can assess the broad range of traits and abilities that help to make a person successful and productive in society, a wonderful person to be around, or even a person of eminence. All tests are imperfect measurers." —JEAN PETERSON

Grades tell only part of the story. The child with high grades might be gifted…or might be a highly motivated, hard-working teacher-pleaser. The child with average or lower grades might have average or lower intelligence…or might be gifted and bored with school.

Teachers might choose the child who's neat, obedient, hard-working, and well-behaved, while ignoring the child who's messy, headstrong, and challenges authority. Not all gifted kids are teacher-pleasers—and not all teacher-pleasers are gifted.

"The extremely bright or the creative, curious, and questioning students, who may be stubborn, rule-breaking, egotistical, or otherwise high in nuisance value, may not be the teachers' favorites, but they sometimes are the most gifted." —GARY A. DAVIS AND SYLVIA RIMM

Parents (that's you) are the real experts on their children but may not know how to go to bat for them. Plus how a child behaves at home may be very different from how he behaves at school. Also, parent recommendation is probably the *least* used way to identify gifted kids. Often, parents aren't even asked.

Important: Once your child gets into the gifted program, that's where he should stay—year after year. Children don't become "un-gifted" from one grade to the next. If your child is "dropped" from the gifted program, find out why. Being identified as gifted one year and not the next is very confusing for a child, plus it can cause serious frustration, anxiety, and loss of self-esteem.

Who gets left out?

When identifying kids for gifted programs, certain groups and types of children are often overlooked and underrepresented. Consider this a heads-up if any of these descriptions fit your child.

Girls. This is more of a problem in middle school/junior high and high school, when many gifted girls try to hide their abilities in order to fit in and feel "normal."

Boys with a lot of energy. They have a hard time sitting still and doing seatwork (paper-and-pencil tasks). Some are so energetic that they are sometimes wrongly believed to have ADD (Attention Deficit Disorder).

Kids with disabilities. Physical, emotional, and/or learning disabilities make it harder for kids to show they're gifted. Meanwhile, adults tend to notice the disability, not the child. Today gifted people with disabilities are called "twice exceptional," but they're still an unseen minority in many schools and communities. Researcher Nick Colangelo has observed that when teacher and parent groups are asked to imagine a "gifted child," they rarely picture one with disabilities.

Troublemakers. Kids who act out, seek attention, disrupt the class, and play the "class clown" are less likely to be identified for gifted programs. In many schools, admission to the gifted program is seen as a "reward," and "bad" kids don't get rewards. But that's confusing behavior with educational need. Gifted children deserve to be in gifted programs because schools should teach *all* children in the way they learn best. What if a physically impaired student acted out in class? Would the school tell him he couldn't use ramps until his behavior improved? Of course not. That's ridiculous. So is keeping kids out of gifted programs if that's where they belong.

Kids from minority or other non-mainstream groups. Many standard IQ and achievement tests are biased in favor of white middle- and upper-class students. They might not measure the skills and abilities of other kids.

Kids who perform poorly on tests. Some gifted kids aren't good test-takers. They get stressed out or are easily distracted and perform below their real capabilities. Or they may have personal problems that get in the way of showing what they know.

Borderline cases. Some kids simply fall between the cracks. Maybe their test scores don't make the cut—but remember, different schools may have different cuts.

Is there a better way?

According to the U.S. Department of Education, schools must develop a system to identify gifted and talented students that:*

- seeks variety—looks throughout a range of disciplines for students with diverse talents
- uses many assessment measures—uses a variety of appraisals so that schools can find students in different talent areas and at different ages
- is free of bias—provides students of all backgrounds with equal access to appropriate opportunities
- is fluid—uses assessment procedures that can accommodate students who develop at different rates and whose interests may change as they mature
- identifies potential—discovers talents that are not readily apparent in students, as well as those that are obvious; and
- assesses motivation—takes into account the drive and passion that play a key role in accomplishment

   We should also think about identifying gifted kids earlier than we do now. Usually children aren't identified until halfway through elementary school. For some, that's too late.

---

* U.S. Department of Education, *National Excellence: A Case for Developing America's Talent,* Washington, DC: 1993.

★

"Most school programs suggest that giftedness isn't identifiable before third or fourth grade. Some schools don't begin to address the abilities of highly able children until middle school or junior high.... By fourth grade, some of the most intelligent children are resentful of waiting for the other kids to catch up. Having learned easy achievement without struggle and persistence, these high-ability students now find little meaning in a school day.... The earliest school years are the most essential for finding these children before their eagerness and joy for learning have been conditioned out of them." —JOAN FRANKLIN SMUTNY, SALLY YAHNKE WALKER, AND ELIZABETH A. MECKSTROTH

★

what You can Do

1. Learn as much as you can about giftedness and what it means. Reading this book is a start, but please don't stop here. See pages 109–115 for more recommendations.

2. Find out if your child's school has a gifted program. In some states, gifted education is *mandated,* meaning that schools are required by law to identify gifted students and provide services for them. In other states, gifted education is *discretionary,* meaning that schools are *allowed* to identify and serve gifted kids but don't have to.

   Note: In recent years, many schools and districts have eliminated their gifted programs. Parents who ask why are told, "There's no money," or "There's no reason to have a special program because all of our children are gifted." It's true that for many schools, budgets are tight. But it's not true that all children are gifted. If you need to discuss this point with a teacher or administrator, you might look back at "What does 'gifted' mean?" on pages 10–11.

3. Start keeping thorough records of your child's achievements and progress in school and outside of school. If you're super-organized, you can set aside folders in a file drawer. If you're not, toss things in a box. Keep all report cards and test reports. Collect examples of your child's work from year to year. This is all evidence you can share with the school if and when it's needed.

4. Keep a daily journal of your child's growth and progress. This doesn't have to be a big deal—jotting a few notes is probably enough for most days. Write down those bright, amazing, funny things he says and does. Track his interests, skills, and achievements. You can also share this with the school. Plus it makes a wonderful gift when your child becomes an adult—a record of his life as a child, seen through a loving parent's eyes.

5. If your child isn't tested at school, have him tested by a psychologist or other trained professional who knows about giftedness and gifted children. If your child goes to public school, you might be able to get the school to pay for the testing. If that's not possible, you might consider bearing the costs on your own, if you can. Here's what one parent has to say:

> "I had my son Daniel tested when he was six years old. It took two days and cost hundreds of dollars, but it was worth it. First, I learned what I had suspected for some time: he has a very high IQ. So I knew I wasn't exaggerating his abilities or his potential, and I knew he belonged in the gifted program at his school. And second, I had 'ammunition' to use when I needed it. I didn't brag about his test results, I didn't tell Daniel about them (to this day, he doesn't know his IQ), and I never shared them with his schools—except once. A teacher suggested that maybe Daniel *didn't* belong in the gifted program. I brought in his scores and showed them to her. End of discussion!"

MYTH: If gifted kids are so smart, they can make it on their own. They don't need special programs.

FACT: This is one of the most popular and troublesome myths about giftedness. It's often used as an excuse for cutting gifted programs or not starting them. *Everyone needs and deserves an appropriate education.* For gifted kids, that usually means something beyond or outside the regular curriculum. Most schools and classes are geared for average learners, not gifted learners. Would you want to spend all day, every day sitting in a classroom going over the same old stuff? Why not teach gifted kids the way they learn best, instead of forcing them to suffer through years of boredom and frustration? Plus appropriate pacing and challenge encourage real learning and develop study skills—which are especially important at higher grade levels and as material becomes more difficult.

A Gifted Program Glossary

As you learn about gifted programming at your child's school, here are some words and phrases you'll want to know.

Acceleration/grade skipping: Advancing kids through grades ahead of the usual age or date. ***Note:*** There's a lot of opposition to grade skipping. People claim that kids suffer emotionally when they're removed from their age group. In fact, studies show that when children are allowed to learn at their own pace, they're *more* motivated to learn, they feel *better* about themselves, and they have *fewer* social problems.

"Keeping a child who can do sixth-grade work in a second-grade classroom is not saving that student's childhood but is instead robbing that child of the desire to learn." —ELLEN WINNER

Cluster class or group: Placing kids in a special class or together in a group in the regular classroom.

Compacting: Compressing several courses or units into a shorter time frame. For example, a child who's a great speller might finish the whole year's spelling lessons in a few months, then move on to more advanced lessons and activities.

Continuous progress: Moving students through the curriculum according to ability rather than grade level.

Differentiation: Modifying the curriculum to meet students' learning needs.

Early entrance: Letting children start kindergarten (or college) before the usual entrance age or date.

Enrichment: Replacing or extending the regular curriculum with special programs that focus on higher-level skills (divergent thinking, problem solving, creativity). Students work with specially trained teachers or community professionals, or they work on their own projects or learning contracts. Enrichment might take an hour a day, an hour a week, or a whole semester. Some communities offer after-school, Saturday, and summer enrichment programs for gifted children. Ask around to see if yours does.

Flexible grouping: Grouping students with similar skills for instruction in a particular subject area, usually math or reading.

Independent study: Letting students work at their own pace on programs that fit their special abilities and/or interests.

Magnet school: A school for gifted children, or for children with special talents or interests (such as French, the arts, or the environment).

Mentorship: Linking a student with a teacher, parent, or older student who acts as a friend, guide, and coach.

Pull-out program: A part-time enrichment program. Students are "pulled out" of the regular classroom for an hour or more each week for extension or enrichment study. *Note:* These programs can be disruptive and imperfect—gifted kids miss out on special events in the regular classroom, and they might be burdened by double homework—but this option is better than nothing.

Resource room: Usually the library (media center) or other specially equipped room that gifted students use at the teacher's discretion. Resource rooms can be havens for gifted kids. On the other hand, there are some schools where the "resource room" is for children who misbehave. Kids spend their 15 minutes (or hour, or longer) staring at a blank wall. Be sure to find out what kind of "resource room" your child's school has.

YOU KNOW YOUR CHILD IS GIFTED WHEN...

She builds a scale model of the Eiffel Tower
out of toothpicks and marshmallows.

42

CREATIVITY

(NO LIMITS)

Creativity is another obvious sign of giftedness. Many artists, musicians, dancers, writers, and other creative types make their gifts public. Showing, performing, and seeing their work in print are part of the fun. A creative child might:

- have an imaginary friend
- enjoy acting and playing "let's pretend"
- spend her free time drawing, painting, writing, sculpting, singing, or dancing
- embellish her artwork with fine details
- make interesting or unusual shapes or patterns using all kinds of materials
- use materials in new and unusual ways
- be open to new and zany ideas
- have lots of ideas to share
- invent words
- make big, dramatic gestures when telling a story or describing something that happened that day
- ask a lot of questions

- respond to questions with a list of possible answers
- think of creative ways to solve problems
- add new details and twists to stories, TV programs, movies, and games
- make up elaborate stories
- make up elaborate excuses for her behavior, or find "loopholes"
- create complicated play and games

When 6-year-old Janet dawdled on her way to school and arrived after the bell rang, the teacher asked why she was late. Janet said, "There was a leprechaun under the hedge and he asked me into his parlor where I found a family of baby mice playing cards, and then...." The story kept building until the teacher called a halt and telephoned Janet's mother. Janet had to stay indoors through three recess periods as a penalty for "not telling the truth." She was confused. "I told the truth," she tried to explain. "What was the truth?" her mother asked. "I had thoughts that made me walk slowly," Janet answered, "and I told my thoughts."

GOOD THINGS: A child with an active, vivid imagination is a joy. Creative kids have endless energy for the things they love to do—dance, paint, pound the piano. They're excellent problem solvers because they can see solutions that rarely occur to other children or even adults. They often grow up to be the artists and performers who enrich our lives, and the visionaries who find solutions to the world's problems.

NOT-SO-GOOD THINGS: A creative child might escape into fantasy, since everyday life seems boring. She might have trouble separating what's real from what's not. She might go off in her own direction instead of following instructions from other people (including you). At school, she might show off. And there's a fine line between elaborate excuses and outright lies.

ways to help your CREATIVE child

1. Encourage and support your child's creativity. Provide her with art materials and other things (games, LEGOs, costumes) to exercise her imagination. Expose her to many types of cultural events (concerts, dances, plays). Sign her up for special classes. Visit museums often and take advantage of the "children's days" or "family days" many sponsor.

2. Make your home a creative place to be. Listen to music. Hang prints on the walls. Have family sing-alongs. Put on skits and plays. Dress up in costumes. Have wild and crazy meals.

3. Set a good example by indulging your own creative impulses. Have you always wanted to play the saxophone or learn the tango? What's stopping you?

4. Let your child decorate her own room (or her own part of the bedroom) however she pleases. (Okay, within reasonable limits.)

5. Make it clear that there are times when you'd love to hear stories, and times when you need to hear the truth.

6. When your child asks a question, no matter how far-fetched it is, never dismiss it as "silly." If you don't have time to address it then and there, tell her when you will—and follow through.

When other little girls were princesses and Power Rangers, Zoë designed her Halloween costumes to be unique. So far, they've included Captain Hook (age 4), Bach (5), Benjamin Franklin (6), Harriet the Spy (8), Wednesday Addams from the *Addams Family* (9), and Hermione Granger from the *Harry Potter* books (10).

To tell or not to tell?

Parents often wonder, "My child has just been identified as gifted. Should I tell her?" In fact, gifted children almost always know they are "different" in some way—just not why or how. If they're not told that they're gifted, and that being gifted is a good thing, they may decide there's something wrong with them. Imagine what a relief it is for kids who think they're "weird" or "stupid" to learn that they're smart and special.

★

"Most gifted children know they are different by the time they are five." —DR. PHILIP POWELL

★

You might think, "Obviously, if my child is in the gifted program, she realizes she's gifted." But what if the program is called something else? Many adults aren't comfortable with the term "gifted," and they worry that kids who are designated "gifted" might get big heads (or that kids who aren't might feel hurt). So gifted programs are called by many different names. TAG, SEARCH, SAGE, STAR, PEAK, REACH, and GATE are some examples.

Should you use the "G-word"? Yes. Kids should know the reason why they think and learn differently from other kids (and feel different, too). Often, gifted kids who are told they're gifted are happy and relieved to learn the truth.

★

"Some degree of 'labeling' is essential if gifted children are to grow up understanding how and why they experience the world differently from others." —DRAPER KAUFFMAN

★

Of course, that doesn't mean your child should go around bragging about being gifted. (Which probably won't happen.) Or that you should go around bragging about how gifted your child is. (Actually, that's probably *more* likely to happen!) Keep things in perspective.

Parents also ask, "Should I tell my child her IQ?" Many teachers and parents think the answer is no. Imagine that you're doing well in school and feeling good about yourself. Suddenly you learn that your IQ is much *lower* than you thought. You might tell yourself, "I guess I'm not that smart after all, so why bother?" Or you find out that your IQ is much *higher* than you thought. You might decide, "I'm so smart that I don't have to study."

Here's what some experts suggest: For now, don't tell. Later, when your child turns 18 or so, ask her if she wants to know her IQ. She might say yes, or she might say no. It might not even matter to her at that stage in her life.

Are gifted kids gifted at everything?

That's what we often expect, but it's not usually how it works. A 4-year-old who reads at a 4th-grade level is still a preschooler. A 6-year-old who wants to save the whales might lose her backpack on the way to school. A 3-year-old who does math problems in his head might struggle to button his coat.

There's a name for this: *asynchronous development*. Gifted kids seem out of sync with what seems appropriate for their age. They may, at times, think like adults and act like children. They seem mature but lack judgment, simply because they haven't been around very long. Sometimes their motor skills lag behind their mental powers. They can see in their mind's eye what they want to do, but they can't get their fingers to cooperate.

When Kendall was 3, her mother found her sitting on the sofa, looking thoughtfully at her feet. "What's up?" her mother asked. "I'm tying my shoes," the little girl replied. "Really?" her mother said. "I didn't know you could tie your shoes." "I can't tie them with my fingers," Kendall said. "So I'm tying them with my thoughts."

Some kids take a wait-and-see attitude, figuring that their motor skills will one day catch up with their mental abilities. For others, asynchrony leads to frustration and outbursts. Be patient and help your child to be patient, too. Reassure her that she'll learn new skills when she's ready.

It's easy to forget that just because gifted children talk like adults, they don't think or feel like adults. And they shouldn't be treated like adults.

★

"Highly gifted children are many ages simultaneously. A 5-year-old may read like a 7-year-old, play chess like a 12-year-old, talk like a 13-year-old, and share toys like a 2-year-old. A child may move with lightning speed from a reasoned discussion of the reasons for taking turns on the playground to a full-scale temper tantrum when not allowed to be first on the swing."

—STEPHANIE TOLAN

★

Don't be surprised if your gifted child follows different timetables in her intellectual, physical, and emotional development. She may have one set of friends who are the same age as she is, and another set of friends who are intellectual equals. She may be able to describe a complex idea in words, yet unable to write it down (or write it legibly). Help her develop her small muscles by playing with play dough or fingerpaints, stringing cereal or beads, or manipulating other small objects. And if you have a home computer, help her learn keyboarding and word processing skills.

YOU KNOW YOUR CHILD IS GIFTED WHEN...

You're exhausted all the time.

HIGH ENERGY

(ALWAYS ON THE MOVE)

Have you ever seen a Looney Tunes cartoon featuring the Tasmanian Devil? This is a creature that splutters, growls, whirls, and buzz-saws his way through life. He moves so fast that he's drawn as a brown tornado. If you look at your child and see "Taz," you know what this characteristic is all about. A child with high energy may:

- stay active until he drops—all day and into the night
- refuse to be idle
- need constant stimulation
- move around a lot, except when focused and concentrating on something that holds his interest
- be restless in mind and body

Note: We generally associate this trait with boys, not girls, since boys seem to exhibit it most often. But there are gifted girls with plenty of energy. And maybe boys show it more because we expect them to be more physically active, while girls are "supposed to be" passive and calm.

Willie, 4, went ice-skating with his aunt Judy. After about an hour of steady exercise, she suggested they take a break and have a snack. "We'd better eat to keep up our energy," she said. "I don't need food to skate," Willie declared. "The energy keeps coming and coming!"

GOOD THINGS: This is a child who can keep up with you and then some. He's ready to go first thing in the morning, and he stays alert in school—as long as he's stimulated and challenged. Plus he's fun to play with.

NOT-SO-GOOD THINGS: A high-energy child is easily bored. If he has to sit still and wait for others to catch up, he might get frustrated and act out. If he doesn't have opportunities to release his pent-up energy, he might squirm in his seat, have trouble paying attention, and refuse to do his schoolwork. Some adults might wrongly assume that he has LD (learning disabilities), ADD (Attention Deficit Disorder), or ADHD (Attention Deficit Hyperactivity Disorder). If this happens, his gifted-ness may go unnoticed because the adults will focus on his learning problem. Plus there's the old misconception that a child with learning problems can't possibly be gifted.

ways to help your ACTIVE child

1. Find healthy, positive outlets for all that energy. Make sure each day includes time for exercise and physical activity. (What a great reason for everyone in your family to get fit and stay fit.)

2. Talk with your child's teacher. Can the children move around during the day? How is excess energy handled in the classroom? Is the teacher sensitive to the needs of high-energy children?

3. Establish soothing, comforting bedtime rituals. End TV time, game time, or other stimulating activities early in the evening. Offer your child a low-protein, high-carbohydrate snack (a banana, an apple, toast and jam, whole-grain cereal) an hour or two before bedtime. Read aloud to him while he's in bed. Then, if he wants, let him listen to relaxing music in the dark, with the volume turned low.

4. If you're told that your child has ADD/ADHD, stay calm. Know that teachers usually aren't qualified to decide if a child has this disorder. (ADD/ADHD is a diagnosis, not an opinion.) Have your child checked out by a doctor. Learn as much as you can about ADD/ADHD. Find out what's really happening in the classroom. And don't be too quick to put your child on medication. That seems to be the right choice for *some* children with attention difficulties, but not *all* children. It's definitely not the answer for gifted children whose real problem is a lack of stimulation in the classroom.

One evening, 7-year-old Kira was too wound up to go to bed. So she read three books. Then she did all of the puzzles in a puzzle book (for ages 9–12). After that, she used the computer to document the family tree. Next, she created and drew a cartoon strip. Then she experimented to see if, when you place a tissue in the bottom of a glass, flip the glass over, stick it into a bowl of water, and then remove it, the tissue stays dry. Still wide awake, she made several origami cranes from memo pads and napkins, and after that she made name tags for the cranes. By then it was 2:30 A.M., and Kira finally turned in for the night.

MYTH: Gifted kids need less sleep than other children.

FACT: Gifted kids need just as much sleep as other children. But because they're so busy thinking, planning, problem solving, and creating, they may have a harder time calming down and going to sleep.

Are there more ways to be gifted?

Howard Gardner, a Harvard psychologist and winner of the MacArthur "Genius" award, believes there are at least eight different ways to be gifted. He calls these "multiple intelligences." They are:

 Linguistic intelligence. Is good with words, language, stories. Is an excellent reader, writer, listener, speaker, speller. Loves memorizing information and building vocabulary.

David, 3, saw a scary movie about ghosts in cemeteries. He decided that "graveyard" was the wrong word; such places should be called "braveyards."

 Musical intelligence. Is sensitive to melody, rhythm, musical patterns, tempo, pitch. May play one or more instruments, with training or by ear. Appreciates many different kinds of music.

Jeanette, 3, was singing a long, involved ballad about frogs and bal-
lerinas. Suddenly her grandmother realized that the melody stayed in
one key, the words rhymed, and they also "scanned"—they were perfectly in sync with the rhythm of the music.

 Logical-mathematical intelligence. Easily learns patterns,
calculations, negotiation skills, numbers, math concepts.
Often enjoys science. Loves games, riddles, puzzles, brain-
teasers, computers.

Shortly after he turned 3, while working his way through the "N" volume
of an encyclopedia, Michael read the section on numbering systems.
He went to his mother and asked her to solve the following equations:
$A - 1 = 1$; $A = 10$. His mother was baffled. Michael grinned and yelled,
"Binary code! Base two!"

Visual-spatial intelligence. Understands how objects and figures relate in three-dimensional space. Can rotate shapes mentally and "see" them from all angles. Enjoys chess, puzzles, LEGOs, maps.

When Luke was 5, he loved drawing maps showing parts of Pasadena, Texas, the city where his family lives. Pasadena is known locally for the way its streets curve around, sometimes even changing names after a curve. To make his maps more interesting (and to see if his parents were really looking at them), Luke would invent streets and add them in. It tickled him when his mom couldn't tell which were the fake streets.

Bodily-kinesthetic intelligence. Is good at handling and manipulating objects. Has excellent body and/or fine motor control. Moves with grace and ease. Excels at crafts. Is a great mimic.

Maria, 4, loved her gymnastics class. One Saturday, after the instructor showed her a new move, she did it twice while he helped her and corrected her technique. On her third try, she did it perfectly with no help. "How could you learn the move so quickly?" the instructor asked. "My body remembers," Maria replied.

 Interpersonal intelligence. Gets along well with others. Understands other people and their feelings. Is a natural leader and born mediator.

When Santa asked Michael, 3, what he wanted for Christmas, Michael spoke quietly and briefly, then hopped down from Santa's lap and toddled back to his parents. "What did you ask for?" his mother asked, hoping it wasn't the Salad Shooter he'd wanted when he was 2. "I told Santa that what I wanted for Christmas was for all the babies in the world to be happy," Michael answered.

 Intrapersonal intelligence. Has keen insight into himself. Manages his own emotions. Sets and reaches goals. Enjoys keeping a journal.

Bobby, 8, struggled with a writing assignment at school. He started three different stories but always got stuck after a few sentences. Finally he finished one, turned it in, and got high marks from the teacher. When he took his story home and gave it to his mother, he told her he wasn't happy with it. "Why not?" his mom wanted to know. "Because it's not a good story," he answered. "I don't have the courage to write down how I really feel."

 Naturalistic intelligence. Has a built-in love of nature. Feels a personal connection to plants and animals. Enjoys being outdoors. Understands how things fit into groups and categories.

Ameli, 9, loves animals. When a proposal arose to create a live animal display in a nearby town, Ameli wrote a letter to the editor in protest. "Animals were not meant to live and die in cage-confined areas," she wrote. In her letter, she also mentioned that animals in the wild die naturally, and their bodies go on to become part of the soil in a continuing cycle of life. The Rocky Mountain Animal Defense League quoted from Ameli's letter in a large mailing, and no one was happier than Ameli when the townspeople voted not to allow caged animal displays.

ways to help your Intelligent child

1. Watch for signs of multiple intelligences in your child. You'll see them.

2. Support and encourage your child's many intelligences, whether you read his stories or listen to his songs, play chess together, shoot hoops, or plant a garden. If your child keeps a journal, *never* read it without permission.

3. Learn more about multiple intelligences. Read Howard Gardner's *Intelligence Reframed: Multiple Intelligences for the 21st Century* (Basic Books, 1999).

4. Learn about another type of smarts. Read Daniel Goleman's *Emotional Intelligence* (Bantam Books, 1997).

5. Share this quotation from Howard Gardner with your child (you may want to make a poster together): "There are hundreds and hundreds of ways to succeed, and many, many different abilities that will help you get there."

6. When you're weary of hearing about test scores and grades, read these wise words by Thomas Armstrong, author of *Awakening Your Child's Natural Genius:* "Forget the standard IQ meaning of genius, and use models like the theory of multiple intelligences to help kids succeed on their own terms."

YOU KNOW YOUR CHILD IS GIFTED WHEN...

She spends four solid weeks studying
Greek and Roman architecture.

FOCUS, PASSION, INTENSITY

(ONE-TRACK MIND)

Gifted children are famously focused. They have incredibly long attention spans for things that interest them—as you probably learned when you tried to drag your child away from a project or game. Or when you announced "Dinner!" for the 10th time to a child whose nose was buried in a book. A child with focus, passion, and intensity may:

- become so involved in what she's doing that she isn't aware of anything else
- throw herself into something; get immersed, even obsessed
- get lost in her own world
- set specific goals and work to achieve them
- collect things
- go further than most kids would to pursue an interest, solve a problem, find the answer to a question, or reach a goal
- take things apart (and put them back together again…maybe)
- concentrate on 2 or 3 activities at one time (the original multitasker!)
- be very observant and not miss a thing
- be very persistent (this child lives by the saying, "If you don't succeed, try, try again")

- ignore any and all distractions (including you)
- stay very interested in one thing, then abruptly switch to another when she has learned what she wants to know

At age 2, Jake already had a passion for cars. He walked the block kicking the tires on all the cars—and every morning, he opened the newspaper, turned to the classified ads, and colored all the car advertisements. By age 3, he could sit on the deck and call out the makes and models of all the cars passing by the house. While sitting in his car seat, still barely able to see out the window, he would endlessly call out, "Toyota Camry...Plymouth Voyager...Buick Park Avenue...Mazda 626...." He loved to attend car shows, where he conversed with the sales people like a pro. He had his own subscriptions to *Motor Trend* and *Auto Week* and was thrilled when the mail carrier delivered a new issue.

GOOD THINGS: Focus, passion, and intensity are *not* character flaws. They're what drive us to do our best, reach our goals, and succeed in life. Some world-changing discoveries have happened by accident, but most have been the result of focus, passion, and intensity.

NOT-SO-GOOD THINGS: A gifted child's passions can lead to stubbornness, tunnel vision, and resistance to interruption. Highly focused children might ignore their chores, homework assignments, family, and friends during periods of white-hot intensity. They have little or no attention span for things that don't interest them. If their passion requires fine motor skills, they might get frustrated when their body isn't up to the task.

ways to help your PASSIONATE child

1. Pay attention to your child's passions. Support and encourage her by providing books and magazines on topics that interest her. Look for related Web sites and explore them together. Introduce your child to other people who share her passions.

2. For the child who loves taking things apart, keep a steady supply of things you no longer need. (What about that old wind-up alarm clock?) Check to make sure they contain no dangerous components such as mercury, lead, or asbestos. Supervise the young child who is working with small parts.

3. Share your passions with your child. Maybe you'll find one (or more) in common.

4. Keep track of your child's school performance. If she's doing brilliantly in only one subject, chances are it's a "passion" and she's neglecting the others. Talk with the teacher. What can be done to make those subjects more interesting to her?

5. Help your child find a balance in life. It's great to have burning interests, and it's thrilling to be caught up in them, but other things are important, too—like family, friends, and time spent having fun or doing nothing.

David, 7, is easily distracted at school. At home, he's able to spend eight hours straight playing computer games such as "Sim Tower" and "Pharaoh"—strategy games designed for teenagers and adults.

What's wrong with perfectionism?

Gifted kids seem especially prone to perfectionism. A few years ago, hundreds of gifted teenagers were surveyed to learn their concerns about growing up gifted. Forty-six percent said they needed help learning how to give themselves permission to fail sometimes. Angela, 17, said, "I personally never felt like anything I did was good enough." Adriane, 12, said, "Many gifted kids are perfectionists, and they always think they can do better."

Often, gifted kids feel pressured by parents, teachers, and friends who expect them to be perfect. These kids are supposed to get straight A's, to know all the answers, and to keep learning as quickly and easily as they always have. As they move through school, however, the material gets harder. If they haven't formed strong study skills, it's not as simple to ace tests as it used to be. These kids are full of anxiety and terrified of failing.

Why is perfectionism a problem? Because perfectionists often:

- set impossible goals for themselves
- limit their options and avoid taking risks
- underachieve (knowing they can't achieve perfection, they give up and stop trying)
- aren't satisfied with their successes
- can't enjoy the moment because they're worried about the future
- are super-critical of themselves and others

- are highly competitive
- are afraid of making mistakes
- are afraid of showing any weakness or imperfection
- procrastinate (knowing they can't do something perfectly, they don't start)
- feel sad, scared, and stressed much of the time
- expect too much of themselves
- expect too much of other people, which makes it hard to have relationships
- suffer from the "impostor syndrome"—the feeling that they aren't really gifted and don't deserve their success

Who wants to live like that? You don't. And your child certainly doesn't.

MYTH: Perfectionism can sometimes be a good thing.

FACT: Perfectionism is *never* a good thing. What's good is the *pursuit of excellence,* which is not the same. Gifted kids (and their parents and teachers) often get the two confused. Perfectionism means that you can *never* fail, you *always* need approval, and if you come in second, you're a loser. The pursuit of excellence means taking risks, trying new things, growing, changing...and sometimes failing.

What You can Do

1. Show your child that you love and accept her "as is"—complete with imperfections.

2. Keep your expectations in check. Make sure they're realistic and humane.

3. Create a safe environment for failure. Give your child permission to make mistakes at home. Don't do everything for her, since this implies that she can't do anything right.

4. Praise your child for taking risks, even when things don't turn out the way she planned. Praise efforts as well as successes. Praise appropriate ways of handling failure. Praise things that have nothing to do with ability. BUT…

5. Don't overdo the everyday praise. This can encourage perfectionism.Plus children who are praised all the time start believing that what they *do* is more important than who they *are.*

6. Get your child involved in activities that aren't graded or judged.

7. Tell your child, "Nobody's perfect. No one is good at everything. That includes me—and that includes you."

8. Tell your child, "Mistakes are for learning." Model the graceful acceptance of your own mistakes. When appropriate, share what you learned from them.

9. When you're about to start something new, talk about things that might go wrong and what you'll do if that happens.

10. Do a perfectionism self-examination. Are you enjoying your own achievements? Or are you too hard on yourself? *Note:* Many perfectionistic children have at least one perfectionistic parent.

★

"The pursuit of excellence is gratifying and healthy. The pursuit of perfection is frustrating, neurotic, and a terrible waste of time."
—EDWIN BLISS

★

PUT-DOWNS VS. POSITIVES

Criticism promotes perfectionism. Are you too critical of your child?

Instead of this...	Try saying this...
"What happened here?"	"How do you feel about your report card?"
"Why can't you do it right?"	"You do a great job of..."
"Why don't you ever..."	"I like it when you..."
"Go look it up."	"Let's find out together."
"That was a dumb thing to do."	"So you made a mistake. What did you learn from it?"
"Act your age."	"I understand how you feel."
"Are you still working on that?"	"Keep trying. Don't give up."
"I told you so."	"Everyone makes mistakes."
"You should have known better."	"What can you learn from this?"
"Just get it done."	"I can see that you're struggling."

Adapted from Sally Yahnke Walker, *The Survival Guide for Parents of Gifted Kids* (Free Spirit Publishing, 1991).

YOU KNOW YOUR CHILD IS GIFTED WHEN...

He arranges all the books in your home
according to the Dewey Decimal System.

LOGICAL THINKING

(STRONG PERSUADER)

Parents of gifted children know what it's like to be talked into a corner. ("He's only six, but somehow he convinced me to let him stay up until midnight on the weekends. He argued his case so well that I just gave in!") The logical thinker may:

- enjoy counting, weighing, measuring, and categorizing objects
- love maps, globes, charts, calendars, and clocks
- enjoy challenging puzzles
- understand money
- prefer his environment to be organized and orderly ("a place for everything, and everything in its place")
- give logical, reasonable explanations for events and occurrences
- come up with powerful, persuasive arguments for almost anything
- want things to be fair, and complain loudly when they aren't
- want things to make sense
- understand cause-and-effect relationships
- want to know reasons for rules

Jake, 3, had always called his dad by his first name, Joe. His mother didn't like this, so she asked her husband to talk with Jake about it. Their conversation went like this:

Joe: "Jake, Mom would really like it if you would call me Dad."

Jake: "Because you're my dad and I'm your son?"

Joe: "Yes."

Jake: "Then are you going to call me Son?"

Joe: "Would you like me to call you Son?"

Jake: "No, I would like you to call me Jake. And I will call you Joe."

GOOD THINGS: You don't have to tell this child to clean his room. He's way ahead of you. His sense of fairness is catching. He's also a strategic thinker, which makes him good at solving problems.

NOT-SO-GOOD THINGS: Watch out! He can spin very believable stories and talk you into almost anything. He might try to organize people as well as things, and people don't like being manipulated. He might need help with his social skills. His way isn't always the "right" way, even if it's logical.

Jeanette, 3½, was angry that she was losing a game of "Pretty, Pretty Princess." Earlier, her father had admonished her for showing poor sportsmanship. As she abruptly left the game, she told her opponent, "I'm not being a poor sport. I've just suddenly lost the desire to be a princess."

ways to help your LOGICAL child

1. Give your child positive ways to use his logical thinking skills. Put him in charge of projects around your home. Let him organize the CDs, videos, or canned goods. Ask him to help plan meals and family events.

2. Are you planning a family road trip? Give your child the maps and ask for his input.

3. When you and your child disagree, take time to hear him out and consider his point of view. Being the parent doesn't make you right 100 percent of the time. Keep an open mind. BUT...

4. Stand your ground when you know you're right, even if your child "out-logics" you.

5. When you must discipline your child, make sure the punishment fits the crime. He won't accept or learn from anything but (you guessed it) logical consequences.

Zachary, 5, was fascinated by his mother's camera—an expensive model with lots of lenses. No matter how often she told him to please leave it alone, she kept finding him with the camera bag open and its contents scattered around him. Exasperated, she asked, "Why can't you just accept that the camera is off limits?" "Because it's for using," he answered. "You're not using it, so why can't I?"

Are young gifted children capable of abstract thinking?

Many are. They think in symbols and pictures. They perceive relationships between people and things. They grasp concepts like death and time. Parents who at first dismiss their child's comments as random cuteness soon realize that the child really "gets it." This is another way in which gifted children may be very different from other kids their age.

Soon after hearing about time machines, 3-year-old Eli asked his mom, "If you and I died, could Daddy use a time machine to see us alive again?" He thought about it some more and added, "You could use a time machine to stop the accident of the ship spilling the oil!"

After watching a TV program on endangered species, Lars, 5, made a poster to protest environmental abuses. At the center was a skull-and-crossbones in a circle with a line drawn diagonally through it. His father asked, "What kind of skull is that?" "It's a cow's skull," Lars explained. "Oh," his dad joked, "I didn't know cows were endangered." "They're NOT, Dad," Lars replied. "The skull is a SYMBOL of death."

How can I help my child make friends?

To a parent, few things are more painful than a child who cries, "I don't have any friends!" We know how important relationships are, and we want our children to know the joys of friendship. We also (let's confess) want our kids to be popular. Or at least well-adjusted socially. "Just not a nerd!" as one parent said.

When gifted kids have social problems, it's usually because they don't have real *peers* to interact with—children with similar interests, abilities, passions, and talents, not just kids the same age. Sometimes, in an effort to fit in, gifted kids pretend to be less smart than they are, which can lead to underachievement.

MYTH: Gifted kids are social misfits.

FACT: Some gifted kids find it hard to get along with children their own age. Their vocabularies are more advanced, and their interests are more sophisticated, intense, and diverse. But they're not social misfits. Gifted kids can form close friendships and lasting, meaningful relationships. They may need adult help finding the right people and developing social skills.

What You Can Do

1. Help your child connect with other gifted kids. Talk with your child's teacher or the gifted program teachers at other schools. Consider joining the National Association for Gifted Children (NAGC) or a state organization dedicated to gifted children. For more information, see page 112.

2. Get your child involved in activities and programs outside of school—groups, clubs, and organizations where he'll meet people who share his interests.

3. Look for science, art, or music classes that mix older and younger children. Some schools combine grades 1–3 and 4–6; see if this is an option for your child. *Note:* This may work for your child when he's in first or second grade, but probably not when he's in third grade.

4. Help your child find a mentor—a caring adult or teenager who will guide and encourage him. For more about mentors, see page 112.

5. Encourage and allow him to have friends of all ages—older and younger.

★

"The term 'peer' does not...mean people of the same age, but refers to individuals who can interact at an equal level around issues of common interest." —W.C. ROEDELL

★

80

YOU KNOW YOUR CHILD IS GIFTED WHEN...

She insists that everyone who visits your home
bring a canned item for the local food shelf.

SENSITIVITY

(FEELS EVERYTHING)

Gifted kids feel more intensely than other children their age. Their emotions seem to range from hysterical laughter to buckets of tears. Many people can accept that gifted kids have adult-like intelligence, but adult-like emotions make them uncomfortable. The child who wins first prize for a report on world hunger is praised, but the child who can't sleep because she's worried about world hunger is viewed with suspicion. (Is she trying to get attention? Being overly dramatic? Or is there something wrong with her?) A sensitive child may:

- have empathy (understanding and awareness of other people's feelings, thoughts, and experiences) at an early age
- have a social conscience at an early age
- quickly pick up on other people's emotions
- be aware of problems that others don't notice
- worry about the world, other people, and/or the environment
- enjoy and respond to beauty
- be very curious about the meaning of life and death

- have an emotional connection to animals (some gifted children are strict vegetarians, even if their families aren't)
- act more emotional than other children her age
- cry, anger, and/or excite easily
- ask many questions about pain, suffering, and/or violence
- respond emotionally to photographs, paintings, and/or sculptures
- respond emotionally to music
- share her feelings and moods through one or more of the arts—music, drawing, painting, sculpture, dance, singing

When Courtney was 6, she and her family went to a restaurant. She ordered juice, and it arrived in a Styrofoam cup. It was barely on the table when Courtney returned it to the waitress, saying politely, "I'm sorry, but I can't drink from this cup." "Why?" the waitress asked. "Do you need a different straw?" "No, thank you," Courtney answered. "The cup is Styrofoam and has chlorofluorocarbons in it, so it's not good for the environment." The waitress didn't blink or laugh—just smiled as she promised to take care of it. She returned with juice in a glass and solemnly vowed not to use Styrofoam cups again.

GOOD THINGS: Because sensitive children know how it feels to be hurt, they're careful with other people's feelings. They might be especially kind and good-natured. They might stick up for friends who are being bullied or teased, and they place high value on helping others. They're responsive and expressive.

NOT-SO-GOOD THINGS: Sensitive children take things personally. They worry about things that are too much for them to handle. They carry the weight of the world on their shoulders and might become fearful, anxious, sad, even depressed. They have trouble handling criticism or rejection. Other people's strong emotions (parents arguing, siblings fighting) make them very upset. They might be extremely picky about what they eat and wear (for example, not tolerating tags, seams, or certain fabrics).

When John was a toddler, he would take off his shoes as soon as his mother put them on his feet. "Why?" she would ask. "My sock hurts," he would say. John couldn't tolerate folds of sock inside his shoe, and the seam had to lie flat in exactly the right spot or off came the sock again. He also couldn't stand the feeling of most sweaters, and all tags in the backs of his shirts had to be removed.

ways to help Your SENSITIVE child

1. Acknowledge and respect your child's feelings. Let her show her feelings in whatever way seems right to her. (It's okay and even good for children to cry—boys included.)

2. Talk about feelings openly and honestly. Share your own feelings when appropriate.

3. Help your child develop a feelings vocabulary. Teach her words she can use to describe all kinds of emotions. The more precisely she can talk about her feelings, the better.

4. If your child feels deeply about the pain, suffering, and plight of others, take this opportunity to do service as a family. You might work at a food bank, visit shut-ins, or volunteer at a children's shelter.

5. Since your child's strong feelings might embarrass her in public, teach her simple ways to gain control of her emotions. Examples: Count slowly from 1 to 10, then backwards from 10 to 1. Breathe slowly and deeply. Think about something happy or silly. *Note:* Be sure to explain that you don't want her to hide her emotions, just "put them away" until she's in a place where she feels more comfortable letting them out.

"Giftedness is a greater awareness, a greater sensitivity, and a greater ability to understand and transform perceptions into intellectual and emotional experiences." —ANNEMARIE ROEPER

When Benjamin was 3, his mother was struggling to make ends meet. As the holidays grew near, she worried that she wouldn't be able to give Benjamin very much. He entered a competition to win a huge Christmas stocking—and he won! The stocking barely fit in their little car. When they got it home and began exploring its riches, Benjamin said, "It's so much, Momma." Then he chose a few of the presents for himself and insisted on taking the rest of them to Penn House, a social service agency in Lawrence, Kansas, so other children could have new toys, too. His mother, touched by his sensitivity and sweetness, asked him why he would give away so much of his bounty. "We have enough, Momma," he said. "And," says his mother, "we did."

THANKS BEN!

PENN HOUSE

How can I help my child handle teasing?

Your child comes home in tears. Why? Because someone teased her for being smart…again.

Gifted kids get teased a lot. Sometimes they can handle it, and sometimes they can't. Sometimes teasing turns into bullying.

If your child tells you she's being teased, treat this as a cry for help. Don't ignore it, and please don't suggest that she "stop being a baby" and fight back. There's already too much violence in our schools and communities.

"In America we often make fun of our brightest students, giving them such derogatory names as nerd, dweeb, or, in a former day, egghead. We have conflicting feelings about people who are smart, and we give conflicting signals to our children about how hard they should work to be smart. As a culture we seem to value beauty and brawn far more than brains." —GREGORY ANRIG

What You can Do

1. Stop what you're doing and really *listen* to your child. Don't dismiss the teasing as "normal." Teasing may happen everywhere, but that doesn't make it normal.

2. Affirm your child's feelings. You might say, "I understand that you feel sad and maybe even angry. Teasing really hurts."

3. Talk with your child about why people tease. In general, these seem to be the main reasons:
   - because they're jealous
   - because they feel threatened and/or inferior
   - because they don't like the person they're teasing
   - because they don't know positive ways to relate and communicate
   - because they think teasing is fun

4. Talk with your child about her experience with teasing. Ask:
   - Who's teasing you?
   - Do you care about this person?
   - Do you care what this person thinks of you?
   - Why do you think this person is teasing you?
   - Are you going to let the teasing bother you?
   - What happens if you do? (You let the teaser determine how you feel.)
   - What happens if you don't? (You take charge of your own feelings.)

5. Practice with your child some ways to handle teasing. Here's one: Stand straight and tall with both feet on the ground. Slowly breathe *in* while counting to three. Then slowly breathe *out* while counting to six. Look the teaser in the eye and say, "I don't like it when you tease me, and I want you to stop." Then walk away.

6. If the teasing is happening at school, encourage your child to talk with the teacher. If the teasing continues, make an appointment to talk with the teacher yourself. Do this right away if you think your child is being bullied. Bullying is a serious problem that must be addressed and stopped.

How can I help build my child's self-esteem?

In recent years, there's been a lot of negative talk and press about self-esteem. If you believe what you hear and read, you may be thinking that self-esteem is a bad thing—that having self-esteem is the same as being conceited or feeling superior to other people.

Kids with self-esteem aren't stuck-up. They're confident and sure. They know their own strengths and weaknesses, feelings and needs. Here's an excellent definition of self-esteem:*

> "Positive self-esteem is the single most important psychological skill we can develop in order to thrive in society. Having self-esteem means being proud of ourselves and experiencing that pride from within. Without self-esteem, kids doubt themselves, cave in to peer pressure, feel worthless or inferior, and may turn to drugs or alcohol as a crutch. With self-esteem, kids feel secure inside themselves, are more willing to take positive risks, are more likely to take responsibility for their actions, can cope with life's changes and challenges, and are resilient in the face of rejection, disappointment, failure, and defeat."

Pride doesn't come from the outside. It comes from the *inside*—from doing things worth being proud of, and being the kind of person others look up to.

---

* Gershen Kaufman, Lev Raphael, and Pamela Espeland, *Stick Up for Yourself! Every Kid's Guide to Personal Power and Positive Self-Esteem* (Free Spirit Publishing, 1999, p. vi).

Building a child's self-esteem isn't about flattery, compliments, and praise. It's about acceptance, affirmation, encouragement, and respect.

Note: Researchers have found that girls ages 8 and 9 are assertive, self-confident, and have high self-esteem. Around age 11, girls' self-esteem starts to fall. They become insecure about their abilities, feelings, looks, and ability to make decisions. If you have a daughter, keep this in mind as she approaches adolescence. Check your library or bookstore for helpful books. One example: *200 Ways to Raise a Girl's Self-Esteem* by Will Glennon (Conari Press, 1999).

Here are five ways to build or boost your child's self-esteem:

1. Let her know that you love her. Show her and tell her every day. Make it clear that you love her *just for herself,* not because she's gifted. Give her the kind of absolute, unconditional love we all need.

2. Tell her specific things you like and admire about her. Go beyond school performance. Does she have a great sense of humor? Do you love her smile? Or the way she helps her little brother pick up his toys?

3. Treat her with respect. Listen carefully when she has something to say. Talk to her with kindness and love in your voice. Try not to shout or yell, even when you're frustrated or angry.

4. When your child makes a poor choice or a mistake, separate the deed from the doer. The *behavior* is bad, not the child.

5. Have family meetings where everyone talks about their accomplishments—things that made them feel proud that week.

YOU KNOW YOUR CHILD IS GIFTED WHEN...

He can always make you smile.

SENSE OF HUMOR

(KEEPS YOU LAUGHING)

Perhaps because they're bright and curious, energetic and emotional, creative and passionate, many gifted kids also have a sense of humor. A child who does may:

- love to laugh
- make up riddles and jokes with double meanings
- understand and enjoy puns and subtle jokes
- "get" jokes that go over the heads of other kids his age
- make up puns
- love all kinds of wordplay (silly definitions, rhymes, words that sound alike)
- laugh uproariously at his own jokes and puns

When Alexa was 4, she was interested in dinosaurs. Her parents got her a placemat describing the various dinosaurs by their ages—Cretaceous, Jurassic, and so on. She was also amused by the words for various bodily functions, including "crepitate"—which means "to make a crackling sound" or, more commonly, "to pass gas." One night she proclaimed, "Daddy's entering the Crepitaceous period!"

GOOD THINGS: What's life without laughter? A sense of humor is essential to our emotional well-being. Sharing laughter with family and friends brings us closer together. Plus studies have found that laughter is good for our physical health. It reduces stress and helps the body fight illness and disease. For gifted kids who feel like nerds or outsiders, being funny can help them feel popular and accepted.

NOT-SO-GOOD THINGS: Brains, verbal skills, and a sense of humor can add up to trouble. Inside every gifted child is a class clown waiting to get out. A child with the power to make others laugh has the potential to be disruptive. Some gifted kids see humor where others don't, and their laughter seems out of place. Their humor may be too advanced for other kids their age, and they get frustrated when others don't "get it." They may not understand or appreciate the silly or "bathroom" humor of other children.

ways to help your HUMOROUS child

1. Talk with your child about humor that's appropriate and humor that isn't appropriate. Some things might be funny at home but not funny at school or the shopping mall.

2. Laugh at your child's jokes. (Yes, even the puns!)

3. If you subscribe to a daily newspaper, read the comics together. Cut out cartoons your family enjoys and post them on the refrigerator or family bulletin board.

4. Go to funny movies, rent funny videos, and watch comedy shows together on TV.

5. Start a family collection of joke books and cartoon books. Encourage your child to write his own joke book and add it to the collection.

6. Find funny books and stories to read aloud at bedtime.

7. Once a week (or once a month), have a family dinner where everyone brings a joke or two to share.

Are there other characteristics of giftedness?

Many or a few, depending on who you talk to or what you read. So far, we've looked at nine that are generally accepted as signs that a child might be gifted:

1. advanced intellectual ability

2. verbal proficiency

3. curiosity

4. creativity

5. high energy

6. focus, passion, intensity

7. logical thinking (and abstract thinking)

8. sensitivity

9. sense of humor

According to the U.S. Office of Gifted and Talented, these are the characteristics of the "typical gifted preschooler" ages 2–5:

- uses advanced vocabulary for age
- uses spontaneous verbal elaboration with new experiences
- has the ability to make interesting or unusual shapes or patterns through various media: blocks, play dough, crayons
- has the ability to assemble puzzles designed for older children
- uses a sense of humor in general conversation
- understands abstract concepts such as death and time
- masters new skills with little repetition
- demonstrates advanced physical skills
- demonstrates advanced reasoning skills through explanation of occurrences

The California Association for the Gifted has this to say:

> "Some children are able to concentrate for long periods of time at a very young age or demonstrate their gifts and talents by using a large vocabulary, constant questioning, creativity, and/or exceptional ability in a particular subject area. Differences commonly found between most gifted learners and their age peers are advanced comprehension, faster pace of learning and a need for school work that provides activities which are both complex and fast paced."

In *Teaching Gifted Kids in the Regular Classroom,* Susan Winebrenner writes, "I believe that any student who possesses most or all of the following characteristics is most probably gifted," then provides this intriguing list:

- learns new material faster, and at an earlier age, than age peers
- remembers what has been learned forever, making review unnecessary
- is able to deal with concepts that are too complex and abstract for age peers
- has a passionate interest in one or more topics, and would spend all available time learning more about that topic if he could
- does not need to watch the teacher to hear what is being said; can operate on multiple brain channels simultaneously and process more than one task at a time

Susan also suggests that gifted students will identify *themselves* if given learning opportunities they appreciate. When that happens in our schools, we won't need lists of characteristics anymore.

If you've read this far, you have an excellent idea of what sets gifted kids apart. Most of all, you have your own intuition or "gut feeling" that your child is special.

Advocating for your gifted child

Maybe your child will have the best possible school experience—classes that meet his learning needs, teachers who challenge him, and opportunities to pursue his interests, thrive, and succeed.

Or maybe not. Unfortunately, most schools are geared for average learners, not gifted learners. Children are placed in programs that match their weaknesses, not their strengths. Chances are you'll have to go to bat for your child—if not now, then at some point during his schooling.

★

"As a parent, you're part of the single largest power-wielding group in the school system, more powerful than teachers or administrators."
—SALLY YAHNKE WALKER

★

Warning Signs

You'll want to stand up and speak out if your child:

- claims to be bored with school or hate school
- tries to get out of going to school (is often sick, too tired to go, doesn't want to go)
- often says he doesn't like the teacher
- says he isn't learning anything in school
- often falls asleep in school
- claims he finishes his school work early and "there's nothing to do"
- is doing too much of the same kind of homework (simple, repetitious "busy work")
- is "learning" concepts, materials, and information he already knows
- starts having self-esteem problems (self-critical, negative, pessimistic)
- shows perfectionistic tendencies or behaviors
- brings home lower and lower grades on assignments and tests
- starts underachieving in school; mentally "drops out"
- brings home reports that he's "not working up to his potential"
- starts perceiving himself as a failure
- doesn't get into the gifted program (if that's where he belongs), or gets dropped from the gifted program (if that's where he's been)

the Basics

Gather as much information as you can. Ask your child about school. What happens during a typical day? What does he like about school? What doesn't he like? What would make school better for him? Get copies of your child's school records. Ask other parents about their experiences and their children's experiences. Learn as much as you can about gifted education in your district and state. Are there laws that affect and protect gifted children?

Decide what you want the school to do. Does your child need more challenge? More stimulation? More chances to follow his own interests? More meaningful homework and less busy work? What do you want the school to do differently? Find out what options are available so you don't ask for the impossible. Talk with other parents.

Keep in mind that schools are bureaucracies and that people often guard their turf. Don't go straight to the principal. This may put the teacher on the defensive. Talk with the teacher first.

Avoid the most common mistakes parents make. These include being confrontive, being impatient, and assuming that teachers, principals, and administrators don't care. This is rarely the case. Also, it helps to remember that no matter how brilliant your child may be, the adults in charge of teaching him still know more than he does.

Ten Tips for Talking to Teachers

1. Make an appointment to meet and talk.

2. If you know other parents who feel the way you do, consider meeting with the teacher as a group. There's strength in numbers.

3. Think through what you want to say ahead of time. Write down your questions or concerns. Make a list of the items you want to cover. You might want to copy your list for the teacher so both of you can look at it during the meeting.

4. Choose your words carefully. Avoid negative, blaming language.

5. Don't expect the teacher to do all of the work or come up with all of the answers. Be prepared to make suggestions and offer solutions.

6. Be diplomatic, tactful, and respectful. Remember that the purpose of your meeting is conversation, not confrontation.

7. Focus on what your child needs, not on what you think the teacher is doing wrong.

8. Don't forget to listen. Be open to what the teacher has to say.

9. Bring your sense of humor.

10. If your meeting isn't the success you hoped it would be, move up a level and try talking to the principal or gifted coordinator. Follow steps 1–9 again. Keep moving up until you get some answers and results.

five Positive Actions You can take

1. Get involved in supporting gifted education. Without parent support, gifted programs wouldn't exist.

2. Offer to help at your child's school. If you can, volunteer in your child's classroom. Then you'll see firsthand what school is like for him.

3. When a teacher makes a special effort to help your child, show your appreciation. Call and say thanks, or send a note or an email.

4. Join (or start) a parent group. In a group, one voice becomes many, and many voices are hard to ignore. You'll also benefit from connecting with parents who know the system and how it works.

5. Attend all parent-teacher meetings.

YOUR RIGHTS AS THE PARENT OF A GIFTED CHILD

- You have the right to know if your child's school has a gifted program. (Even if they call it by another name.)
- You have the right to know if your child is in a gifted program or class.
- You have the right to know how children are identified for the gifted program. (Tests? Observation? Assessment? A combination?)
- You have the right to know when children are tested for the gifted program and what tests are given.
- You have the right to know your child's test results and what they mean. (If the results are confusing or hard to interpret, ask for help.)
- You have the right to know what kind of training teachers in the gifted program receive. (Also, how are teachers selected for the program?)
- You have the right to know if the gifted program at your child's school is working. Ask how the program is evaluated. Ask to see the results of the latest evaluation.
- You have the right to ask questions and get answers.
- You have the right to visit your child's school and the gifted program.
- You have the right to be a "pushy" parent—if being "pushy" means exercising your rights and advocating for your child.

Taking care of yourself

"My teacher said we shouldn't be too proud that we're smart—that we got our brains from our parents. But in the newsletter for parents of gifted kids, it says it's very difficult to take care of a gifted child. So why do parents make us smart if it just makes their job tougher?" —GIRL, 8

It's estimated that there are between 2–3 million gifted children in the United States alone. Worldwide, gifted kids comprise maybe 5 percent of the population.

So you're not alone. Take comfort in that—and take care of yourself, because you're going to need your strength, wits, and wisdom in the months and years ahead as you do the tough work of raising a gifted child.

But even if your child is the most profoundly gifted person in the history of the world, parenting is only part of who you are. Some moms and dads literally live for their gifted kids. There's more to life! Love your child. Do your best to meet his needs at home. Spend time together. Try your best to get him an education that's stimulating, rewarding, and satisfying. Be there for him. And make time for yourself.

Regularly set aside a half-hour or an hour just for you. Read a book or magazine. Take a walk. Call a friend. Take a nap or a bubble bath. When you take care of yourself, you teach your child to do the same.

Start a new hobby or go back to one you've neglected. Maintain your friendships with other adults. Ask for help when you need it. Look for humor where you can find it—studies have shown that healthy families laugh a lot. And never forget that parenting a gifted child has its own rewards, and they're priceless. In the words of one parent:

> "One of the best parts of life with a gifted 2-year-old has been hearing her day-to-day observations—ones that make us stop our busy lives for a moment to see the world from her point of view. Noticing a metal clothesline pole, she says in excitement, 'It's a big letter T!' Holding up half an apple slice, she comments, 'It looks like a sailboat.' This winter, while we were sitting in a traffic jam on the highway, she remarked, 'Mom, look at the butter trees over there.' I looked, and across the sea of cars, the winter tree branches were covered with a layer of fresh snow."

Resources for Parents and Teachers

Books

Alvino, James. *Parents' Guide to Raising a Gifted Child* (New York: Ballantine Books, 1996). A practical guide to raising and educating gifted children.

Clark, Barbara C. *Growing Up Gifted: Developing the Potential of Children at Home and at School* (New York: Prentice Hall, 1997). One of the most interesting, information-packed introductions available to the characteristics of gifted and talented children.

Galbraith, Judy. *The Gifted Kids' Survival Guide for Ages 10 & Under* (Minneapolis: Free Spirit Publishing, 1999). A classic introduction to growing up gifted, revised and updated. Written to and for gifted kids, but parents and teachers can read it, too.

U.S. Department of Education, Office of Educational Research and Improvement. *National Excellence: The Case for Developing America's Talent* (Washington, DC: 1993). A conclusive, easy-to-understand report on gifted children's educational needs. Call toll-free 1-877-4-ED-PUBS (1-877-433-7827) to request a copy. Or find it on the Web *(www.ed.gov/pubs/DevTalent/)*.

Rimm, Sylvia. *Keys to Parenting the Gifted Child* (Hauppauge, NY: Barrons Educational Series, 1994). How to work with schools, manage problems, and advocate for your child.

Saunders, Jacqulyn, and Pamela Espeland. *Bringing Out the Best: A Guide for Parents of Young Gifted Children* (Minneapolis: Free Spirit Publishing, 1991). Hundreds of ways to promote creativity and intellectual development—without pushing.

Smutny, Joan Franklin, Kathleen Veenker, and Stephen Veenker. *Your Gifted Child: How to Recognize and Develop the Special Talents in Your Child from Birth to Age Seven* (New York: Ballantine Books, 1991). Helps parents and educators understand the characteristics and needs of young gifted children.

Smutny, Joan Franklin, Sally Yahnke Walker, and Elizabeth A. Meckstroth. *Teaching Young Gifted Children in the Regular Classroom: Identifying, Nurturing, and Challenging Ages 4–9* (Minneapolis: Free Spirit Publishing, 1997). Written for educators (and parents) who believe that *all* children deserve the best education we can give them.

Walker, Sally Yahnke. *The Survival Guide for Parents of Gifted Kids: How to Understand, Live With, and Stick Up for Your Gifted Child* (Minneapolis: Free Spirit Publishing, 1991). What giftedness means, how kids are identified as gifted, how to advocate for your child at school, and more.

Webb, James T., Elizabeth A. Meckstroth, and Stephanie S. Tolan. *Guiding the Gifted Child: A Practical Source for Parents and Teachers* (Scottsdale, AZ: Gifted Psychology Press, 1989; updated 1995). A classic, packed with parenting techniques and information to help you help your gifted child.

Winebrenner, Susan. *Teaching Gifted Kids in the Regular Classroom: Strategies and Techniques Every Teacher Can Use to Meet the Academic Needs of the Gifted and Talented,* revised edition (Minneapolis: Free Spirit Publishing, 2000). Read this book to discover *many* ways to meet the learning needs of gifted students in the mixed-abilities classroom.

Winner, Ellen. *Gifted Children: Myths and Realities* (New York: Basic Books, 1997). A psychology professor examines the latest scientific evidence about the biological basis of giftedness, as well as the role parents and schools play in fostering exceptional abilities.

ORGANIZATIONS

The Association for the Gifted (TAG)
The Council for Exceptional Children (CEC)
1920 Association Drive • Reston, VA 20919-1589
1-888-CDC-SPED (1-888-232-7733) • *www.cec.sped.org*
Provides information to professionals and parents about gifted and talented children and their needs. TAG is a division of CEC, and you must be a CEC member to participate. If you visit the CEC Web site, click on <u>Eric Clearinghouse on Disabilities and Gifted Education</u>, then on <u>Gifted Education/Dual Exceptionalities</u> for a directory of Frequently Asked Questions (FAQs) files, digests, fact sheets, and links.

National Association for Gifted Children (NAGC)

1701 L Street, NW, Suite 550 • Washington, DC 20036

(202) 785-4268 • *www.nagc.org*

A national advocacy group of parents, educators, and affiliate groups united in support of gifted education. Join to receive the quarterly magazine *Parenting for High Potential,* discounts on selected NAGC publications, and more. NAGC has affiliates in every state.

The National Mentoring Partnership

1400 I Street, NW, Suite 850 • Washington, DC 20005

(202) 729-4345 • *www.mentoring.org*

A resource for mentors and mentoring initiatives across the United States. Visit the Web site to learn more about mentorship. The site also lists many local and national organizations that connect mentors with kids and kids with mentors.

Supporting the Emotional Needs of the Gifted (SENG)

405 White Hall • Kent State University

PO Box 5190 • Kent, OH 44242-0001

(330) 672-4450 • *monster.educ.kent.edu/CoE/EFSS/SENG/*

Directed by Dr. Mary Landrum, SENG helps parents identify giftedness in their children and helps children understand and accept their unique talents. It also provides a forum for parents and educators to communicate about effective ways to live and work with gifted individuals.

David C. Baird's Gifted Children Web Site

home.ican.net/~agtechn/

Thoughts and advice from people who have spent years identifying gifted children, working with them, and helping them define themselves, their strengths, and their role in society.

Gifted and Talented (TAG) Resources Home Page

www.eskimo.com/~user/kids.html

Links to all known online gifted resources, enrichment programs, talent searches, summer programs, gifted mailing lists, and early acceptance programs, many years' worth of mailing list archives, and information about local gifted associations and government (mostly U.S. state) programs.

The Gifted Child Society

www.gifted.org/

This nonprofit organization provides educational enrichment and support services for gifted children, assistance to parents, and training for educators. Since 1957, the Society has served over 50,000 children and their families. In 1975, the U.S. Department of Education named it a national demonstration model.

Gifted Children

www.gifted-children.com/

Gifted Children Monthly, a multi-award-winning newsletter "for the parents of children of great promise," has ceased publication—and returned as Gifted-Children.com, a networking and information site.

GT World

www.gtworld.org/

An online support community for parents of gifted and talented children. Look for articles, links, testing information, definitions, three mailing lists, and an area where members can talk to each other in real time.

Hoagies' Gifted Education Page

www.hoagiesgifted.org

Much more than a "page," this is a wide and respected variety of resources for parents and educators of gifted youth, from research to everyday success stories, personal support groups, and links.

Jon's Homeschool Resource Page

www.midnightbeach.com/hs/

One of the oldest, largest, and most popular homeschooling sites on the Web. Start by reading the homeschooling handbooks and answers to Frequently Asked Questions, contact a support group in your area, and subscribe to the mailing list.

State Resources for Gifted Education

ericec.org/fact/stateres.htm

A list of State Department of Education offices responsible for gifted education and statewide advocacy groups, with contact information and links (where available). Advocacy groups offer members a variety of services including parent support groups.

TAG Family Network

www.teleport.com/~rkaltwas/tag/

Run by and for parents, this organization is dedicated to education and advocacy for gifted and talented youth. It provides information, supports parents, and monitors and influences legal issues. The Web site contains current information on gifted education, with links to other sites of interest to parents, educators, and children.

TAG: Families of the Gifted and Talented

www.tagfam.org/

An Internet-based support community for talented and gifted individuals and their families. Read the articles and join one or more of the mailing lists.

INDEX

About the Author and Illustrator

Judy Galbraith, M.A., has a master's degree in guidance and counseling of the gifted. She has worked with and taught gifted children and teens, their parents, and their teachers for over 20 years. In 1983, she started Free Spirit Publishing, which specializes in Self-Help for Kids® and Self-Help for Teens® books and other learning materials.

Judy is the author of *The Gifted Kids' Survival Guide for Ages 10 & Under.* She is also the coauthor of *The Gifted Kids' Survival Guide: A Teen Handbook* (with Jim Delisle, Ph.D.), *Managing the Social and Emotional Needs of the Gifted* (with Connie Schmitz, Ph.D.), *What Kids Need to Succeed: Proven, Practical Ways to Raise Good Kids* (with Peter L. Benson, Ph.D., and Pamela Espeland), and *What Teens Need to Succeed: Proven, Practical Ways to Shape Your Own Future* (with Peter and Pamela).

Ken Vinton, M.A., is the author/illustrator of *Alphabetic Antics* and *Write from the Edge* and has illustrated several other books. He teaches art to 7th–9th graders in Pennsylvania and works with gifted students in the area of creativity. He also teaches art education at Indiana University of Pennsylvania. Ken and his wife are the parents of two gifted grown-ups, a son and a daughter ages 19 and 21.